THE
WARRIOR WAY

HOW TO BATTLE SATAN AND WIN EVERY TIME.

LEANNE MCDOUGALL

authorHOUSE®

AuthorHouse™
1663 Liberty Drive
Bloomington, IN 47403
www.authorhouse.com
Phone: 1 (800) 839-8640

Published by AuthorHouse   09/21/2015

ISBN: 978-1-5049-2553-2 (sc)
ISBN: 978-1-5049-2554-9 (e)

Library of Congress Control Number: 2015912096

Print information available on the last page.

Contents

Acknowledgements

This book is to all the Warriors out there that spend time battling Satan. I know at times you feel like you are standing alone, but just know you have a mighty army standing with you.

I also want to express my deep gratitude and appreciation to my 5th and 6th grade Sunday School Class. Your love for the Bible and your longing to know Jesus more is such an inspiration to me. You are like little sponges and you keep me alert and on my toes. You challenge me to be ready with an answer on any given Sunday. You are truly Warriors!

Next, I would like thank my friend Becky for being such and encouragement to me and being the first to implement the skills I outlined in this book. I also thank my mom for the endless hours she worked with me to make this book a reality. And of course, I cannot forget my incredibly gorgeous husband who has been my best friend and my sounding board for years. I totally know I am a Rock Star in his eyes and I Love it!

Finally, to my dad. Thank you for showing me that standing up for what I believe in is honorable. Thank you for showing me Jesus. You were always my warrior.

Warriors, I salute you!

CHAPTER 1

Under Attack

*¹² For we do not wrestle against flesh and blood, but against
principalities, against powers, against the rulers of the
darkness of this age, [a] against spiritual hosts of wickedness
in the heavenly places. Ephesians 6:12 (NKJV)*

The room was dark and stale. There seemed to be an
essence in the air that lingered in such a way as to make my
skin tingle with fear. The bed beneath me was damp from a
sudden burst of sweat that raced from my body. My heart was
beating so loud that it overpowered my hearing. Sounds were
muffled and muted. There was a persistent ringing in my ears
that no matter how hard I focused on making it diminish, it
would not let up. I wanted to speak, but I was unable to open
my mouth. I wanted to get out of bed, but I was glued to the
mattress, too paralyzed to move. I closed my eyes and tried to
think this hellish scene away, but closing my eyes only made
the nightmare worse.

I saw myself in a dusky room with an eerie red glow that
seemed to come out of nowhere. Crouching in the corner
in a fetal position, I raised my hands over my head in a

1

frantic attempt to protect myself from a severe beating. I was whimpering and weeping, cornered by a vicious predator. I focused my mind's eye on the scene, and then the haze disappeared. I was able to witness my attacker as if I were an onlooker watching from a short distance. The demon was a ghoulish nightmare of a creature that had a crooked back and gray, leathery skin. It frightened me just to look at him. He had a club in his hand, and he was beating me. He would raise his boney hand above his head and bring the club down on top of my arms.

At the same time he was hitting me, he was screaming curses at me. "You are worthless. You have nothing to offer anyone. You will never succeed. You are going to lose everything you love. You are a fool. God is so angry with you for all the mistakes you have made. You will never be able to recover from your mistakes. I don't know why you try so hard. You are always going to fail. You always thought that God had given you gifts, but He has given you nothing. You always try your best, but I am here to tell you that your best will NEVER be good enough! You might as well just GIVE UP! YOU ARE A FAILURE!"

As this creature was beating me, I heard whispers coming from my lips. "Please…" I said breathlessly. "Please stop." I continued on with my plea. "Please, stop. This is more than I can bear. Have mercy." My whimpers were ignored and yet I kept calling out, "I am dying and I cannot breathe. Please…. I beg you, please stop." My pathetic cry for relief was falling on deaf ears. I was begging for mercy from a creature who had none to give. I was looking for a light of hope from a creature whose job was to steal any hope I had. I sat there motionless on the floor as I allowed this demon to overpower my mind and my emotions.

Suddenly, I heard a thunderous voice in my mind. It was a voice of authority and command. "GET UP!" said the voice with strength and confidence. I didn't know who the voice was talking to, so I questioned, "Who me?"

"Yes, you!!" The voice sent chills through my body.

I protested, "I cannot. I am overcome by this devil and I cannot move. I will die if I move."

"You will surely not die. Get up!"

At that moment the demon began to beat me even harder. The sound of his cursing became more frantic and grimacing. The level of intensity grew as he continued to scream curses in my direction. I flinched from being scorched by his escalating anger.

Then I hear a voice of authority say to me, "Get Up!"

Terrified and desperate I screamed, "I do not know how to get up. I am afraid. I cannot move."

The voice of God called to me saying, "You can move. You are more powerful than this demon who is torturing you. Don't let him hit you again! Get up!!"

The demon paused for just a moment, and I thought I saw a glimpse of distress in his eye. I was not certain because he continued his chanting and his beating of me.

"I do not know how to get up. Lord, please tell me what I should do?"

God whispered to me, "Call upon my Son. Say the name Jesus."

"Jesus?" I thought to myself, as the demon continued his rampage.

"I said, say the name Jesus. Out loud. Say it loud for the whole world to hear."

"Jesus?" I whispered, questioning how this could be the answer to this great thrashing that was being leveled upon me.

Suddenly, everything transitioned in front of my eyes. The demon stopped in his tracks. He folded over in pain as if something or someone had just delivered a great blow to his gut. I wasn't sure what was happening, but I knew mentioning this name had temporarily stopped the beating I had been taking just a moment before. So I tried it again.

"Jesus." I said, with a little more confidence, now standing to my feet, hoping that this devil would respond the same way as he had before. This time the creature's eyes widened with terror and he raised his club to hit me again. I screamed, "Jesus, Jesus, Jesus! YOU HAVE TO LEAVE ME ALONE

BECAUSE OF JESUS!!!" The demons body contorted and his mouth widened as he dropped the club he was beating me with, and in a flash he immediately disappeared.

The nightmare was over, and I opened my eyes. I was now able to move again and breathe. I had been holding my breath, for who knows how long, and my heart was racing at top speeds. When I opened my eyes, I realized that I was saying the name of Jesus right there as I lie in my bed. It was over. The fight was over, and Jesus had won. Praise be to God! The night of hell was over, or was it?

I immediately began to feel the attack of the enemy reenter the room with me. No sooner had the attacker returned when I heard the voice of my Father say, "Leanne, be at peace. I AM here with you. Be calm and know that I AM your God." Instantly, a sense of tranquility rushed over my body. I relaxed and lay there in calmness while I heard my Savior continue to talk with great kindness, saying, "Daughter, Satan has come to kill, steal and destroy. He will not snatch your salvation because you are secure in me. He will try to destroy your life here on earth, if you listen to him and allow him to manipulate you. I AM here to tell you that he has NO authority over you. The only control he has over you is the control you willfully hand over to him. You can win these battles. In fact, you have already won through me. But you are going to have to find out who I really AM, if you are going to win all of these battles every time. This emotional roller coaster you are living on is not faith. You will never have complete victory in your life until you find out what is true faith. You will not have full victory until you discover how to fully live in Me.

I replied, "I know that your words are truth, but I just don't know how to do what you are saying. How is it possible to genuinely believe in something I cannot see and be certain of what I hope for? It seems like this world is so harsh and unpredictable. I went to bed last night with the words out of Proverbs: Hope deferred makes the heart sick. God, my heart is so sick. I feel like it is almost dead. I just don't know how to do what you are asking of me."

God said, "I know sweetheart. That is why I AM here. I will show you how to trust in Me. We will take this journey together. Now is the time to rest."

*****

I remember that night very vividly. It was a night filled with fear and distress. It was a cosmic battle that I had undergone early in my life. A night that transformed my life forever. Night terrors were not always a part of my life. I was born and raised in the loveliest of homes. I had a caring mother and a loving father. My brother was my best friend, and I slept in warmth and happiness with my favorite dog all of my young life. Growing up, I was taught about Jesus and I was constantly reminded about how much Jesus loved me. My father would always talk about the loveliness and power of grace, and I thought I knew what he was talking about until my time of testing came.

Somewhere along this adventure called life, I came under the impression that it was not only my responsibility to "love" God, but to impress Him. I needed to improve His opinion of me. The most efficient way of accomplishing this task was through my actions and my good works that I would perform for Him. Things like doing daily devotions and praying at least 15 to 30 minutes a day were the minimum requirements. More would be better, but never less. When I fell short of these minimum requirements, I found myself spending a great deal of time repenting and praying for forgiveness. I was afraid I would lose my favor with God. I would occasionally work through a bible study or two, just to make sure that my life was continually going in the right direction. Volunteering was an excellent opportunity to get a few more bonus points with God. Therefore, I participated in as many activities as I could. After all, I was here to do God's work. God needed me to be His hands and feet. I had to prove to God that I was worthy enough for Him to use me in His ministry. I was so busy doing God's work, and my mind was so full of activity and opinions that I was unable to actually hear God's Spirit trying to communicate with me. Most of the time I was unaware of that still, small voice inside of me that was speaking every day.

The problem with this philosophy of "doing good to get God's approval", is that it works reasonably well as long you are living your life in a seemingly "good" manner. If there are no major catastrophes or screw ups, a person can live in this manner with a fair amount of satisfaction and contentment. However, most of us have found that life is not trouble free. Many of us fail at one point or another, and many times we fail miserably. Life is unpredictable, and sometimes we make a poor choice that takes us in the opposite direction of our initial objective. So then what? What happens when you fall flat on your face, and you make every mistake that you just knew you would never make? The problem with trying to impress God or trying to "earn" His love is that when you are doing good there is a reasoning that God is happy with you, and that He loves you and is blessing you. When you haven't done so well, or life gets rough, it only stands to reason that God is now angry with you. He is willing to withhold His blessings until you get it right. It is the "Do good, get good and do bad, get bad" philosophy. Even if you know that God loves you no matter what, there is a sense of despair at the thought that God, whom you love so much, is angry with you and is punishing you. It can become such a deep seated sense of despair that it becomes impossible to pull yourself out of this pit. It is completely impossible except for one factor… His Grace.

The deepest moment of my despair was on a Sunday morning, when I found myself kneeling on my bedroom floor weeping. I was crying out with a terrible agony clenching my heart. I was asking my husband why I was unable to pull myself out of this dark, dark place. There seemed to be a gloomy cloud always hovering over my head. Even after I was on an anti-depressant and under a doctor's care, I was unable to escape the emotional roller coaster that seemed to dominate and control my life.

Suddenly, while kneeling next to my bed, I had an epiphany. I had a revelation so clear and pure that it made me angry that I had been ignoring it for so long. I said to my husband, in a voice of resentment and frustration, "Jeff, this is not Faith!" I continued on, "This up and down wave of emotions I am living on is NOT FAITH." A lightbulb switched on in my mind, "That is it! I need faith. I need God's Faith. I guess I don't know what real Faith looks like or how to even achieve it. I am making it my life's mission, starting today, to find out what Faith is and live in it!" Jeff looked at me a bit stunned. I suppose it was a bit shocking for him to hear my honest confession. Here I was a young woman, born and raised in the church, pursuing God in every way I knew how, coming right out and confessing, "I do not have Faith." However, immediately, his shocked look was replaced with a gentle smile as he said to me, "Then we will take this journey together."

It didn't solve any of my problems instantaneously, but at least there was a spark of hope. It was a place to start. Even though I did not know how to achieve this objective, I now knew what the answer was. It truly gave me something to hold on to. I didn't realize how important the timing of that decision was until three days later when I faced the first of many painful tests on this journey.

Chapter 2

A Man of Honor

6 Humble yourselves, therefore, under God's mighty hand, that he may lift you up in due time. 7 Cast all your anxiety on him because he cares for you. 1 Peter 5:6-7

"Hey Inky, do you want to go to work with me today."

"Yes, please!" I answered my father with great delight. Going to work with my dad was a highlight in my life. Dad just knew how to make everything special. I would crawl into his work van on a very cold and dreary day. The rain could be pouring down, the fog so thick that you could not see two feet in front of you, and he would inevitably say, "Look! It's clearing up. See, the sun is peeking through the clouds." All my life I would look intently for the sun. Even though I rarely could see any indication of the sun on such burdened and overcast days, I would always believe him. He would say it with such conviction and confidence, I knew it must be true. I never doubted that the sun was just about to peek through the gloomiest of storms. I would just wait in anticipation for the glorious arrival of the sun. Sometimes it would take days for the sun to appear, but remarkably, my father was always right. The sun would always break through the most dreadful of storms and the darkest of days.

It wasn't until I was older that I realized that people would laugh "at" my dad when he would say such silly things. In younger years I always thought that they were laughing "with" him. But one day I realized that some weren't laughing "with" him, as in a friendly gesture of agreement. They were laughing "at" him, as if to say, "Dan, there is no sunshine anywhere to be seen on such a terrible day. Today is just a sad, dreary day that no amount of optimism is going to cure."

To be honest, I was shocked when I realized that others didn't share my father's belief that the sun was just about to make its appearance. To me, just the thought that the sun was ready to break through made the day so much brighter. Our family lived in cloudy days as if the sun was shining bright. We would play and sing and work as if there was a sun, then suddenly there was. It was a glorious way to live life, and I loved it. Until the day came when I couldn't see the sun, even when it was shining bright outside for all to see.

My father continued to be the joy of my life. He always had a spark of happiness, and he was truly the silver lining to every cloud. Now I had a family of my own, and the pressures of life were screaming out to me loud and clear. I knew, profoundly, that I had made imperfect choices, and my choices were bearing down on me. I had huge regrets. I was afraid that I was failing in all my responsibilities as a mother and wife and as a Christian. My sense of failure or potential failure was heavy upon me. I felt like everywhere I turned and every door I opened, I could never get away from the cloud of darkness that seemed to consume me. The only time I would feel moments of relief was when I was completely focused on the beauty of my children and when I was with my Mom and Dad.

Jeff, my husband, was my rock during this time of my great need. He was patient with me and in constant prayer for me. I knew he felt helpless in his attempts to comfort me, but he never stopped trying. My mom was my best friend, and I talked to her all the time. I would pour my heart out to her until the confusion in my mind would come clear. Sometimes, even though the foggy thoughts never became clear, our heart-to-heart chats would always bring some relief. My dad, however, was my sunshine. The times spent with Dad were the moments I felt life was pure and simple. The sunshine in his life brought sunshine to my life. It penetrated through my darkness and touched my soul. His touch on my life kept me going and gave me something to smile about. That might explain why, for four years of my life, rarely a day went by that I would not find myself at my parents' house for a cup of coffee. Sometimes, it was twice a day.

The day we found out my dad was sick was the day I severed my emotions altogether. I shut everything down and divorced myself from all feelings. A self-imposed lobotomy is very much how I would describe my reaction to the word "cancer". I knew my mom and dad would think that I was being thoughtless and careless about this devastating news our family was receiving, but I could not do anything about it. I was paralyzed. To think about what was happening would destroy me. I seemed uncaring. To care would take me into a state of despair that I was afraid I would never return from. I knew that if I didn't shut myself down I would be lost. I still loved my dad dearly, I was just afraid to care.

He was the most courageous man when facing this disease. He would say that he had a fight on his hands, and, boy, did he fight. Dad began to pray. He not only would pray, but he would believe. A bad report would come and he would say, "That might be so…, but my life is in the healing hands of God." He was such an inspiration and he NEVER gave up. He lived life to its fullest every day. Watching him battle like a fearless warrior was inspiring to me. I began to pray like he was praying, and I found myself believing like he was believing. He never stopped living his life to the fullest. He was inspiring us all, but not really surprising us. His attitude to the cancer was very uncommon and unusual compared to the average reaction we had witnessed. However, Dad's response was not unusual for him. This is the way Dad had faced all his trials in life, with the true belief that God was in control and that nothing was a surprise to God. Dad's life was in God's hands, and Dad never let us forget that.

In the middle of one of his treatments, he took the time to train for and complete a 200-mile bike ride. He wanted to take this journey with me and my brother. Living life's experiences with his family was always a priority to him. The training was slow and constant, and his mission was accomplished with wondrous success. Dad rode his first 200-mile bike ride, just following one of his corrective surgeries designed to fight off his cancer. The journey was magical and victorious. It was inspiring to everyone who had the privilege of participating in the ride with him.

A couple of years had passed, my emotional state was equalizing, but I was still far from gaining true victory. I was learning how to live from happy moments to happy moments. Then came the night of great torment. Satan attacked me hard that night. I was paralyzed and frightened. There seemed to be nothing I could do to protect myself from the vicious attack of a heartless and merciless demon. Then I heard the voice of God tell me to, "Get Up!" At that moment, my life began to change. I found myself desiring to not only impress God but to truly listen for the voice of God. I got up the following morning and declared that I was going to start a great and worthy journey to find out what is true faith was. I was still sad, but now I had hope.

During all of this emotional and spiritual kafuffle, my dad and I decided that we were going to start training again for our notorious 200-mile bike ride. He wanted me to train for it with him. Three days after I had made the declaration that I was going to discover true faith, through the leading of God, I woke up as depressed as ever. My sadness was permeating, and I was angry that yet another day of gloom was to consume me. Then I remembered, with a start, that I was supposed to be on a ride with Dad. I called to see if he was waiting for me, and he was not. He thought I wasn't going, so he left on his training without me. I was mad and frustrated that I had forgotten, so

I was going to sit down and pout. Then I jumped up and said, "This is not going to have control over me!" I jetted out of the door and jumped onto my bike. I began to peddle as fast as I could in an attempt to catch up with Dad. The day was cloudy and the moisture in the air was so heavy it began to drizzle. I laughed at the thought of me and Dad riding our bikes in this inclement weather. It was par for the course. This was the life we lived, present to the moment and not letting anything, including weather, stand in our way. I found joy at thinking of how Dad and I would laugh at ourselves for forging through yet another rain storm.

At that point, the most unusual thing happened. I heard the faint sound of sirens in the distance. I automatically assumed the source of the sirens was somewhere in the canyon or on some distant road. I was so startled when the sound grew louder and more pronounced until the ambulance itself raced past me. Again, I thought to myself that Dad and I were going to have so much to talk about on the bike ride home. First, there was the rain, and then the curiosity of an ambulance up in our neck of the woods.

It never dawned on me for even the slightest second that the ambulance was racing to save my dad's life. Just before I came on the scene, there were two kind and gentle looking men approaching me. They were coming to warn me that there was an accident with a bike rider, and they thought that the man on the bike was dead. My heart lodged in my throat. I grabbed the chest of the man who was communicating this information to me.

I said, "Did you say a man on a bike?" I am sure the horror in my eye depicted all the fear that was inside of me. The two men began to back track and say, "Well, we are not certain that he is dead. The paramedics are working on him now. Do you know him?"

"I think he is my dad."

"Sweetheart, it might not be him. He is not dressed like you." I chuckled, because my dad never dressed like a biker. He always dressed like a farmer on a bike. We often would make fun of his attire. Many times he was the source of great entertainment. Even though I chuckled, the statement made it more evident that this man, whose life these people were trying to save, was my father.

I walked up to the scene, and my greatest fears were confirmed. It was him. He was lying lifeless in the ditch, and there were men around him working in a controlled manner, trying to save his life. It was a surreal moment. To these men, they were performing their job and doing it very well. To my father, he was experiencing the beginning of eternity. To me, my life was crumbling before my eyes. This couldn't be happening.

I was kneeling on the ground with my face in my hands. I was trying to catch my breath. My mind was reeling and trying to sort out what I was supposed to do. I knew I needed to let my mom know what was happening, but in my rush to get out of the house, I had left my cell phone at home. Then, what seemed out of nowhere, a lovely lady grabbed my arm.

"How can I help you? Do you know this man?"

"Yes, he is my father. I need to call my mother, and I don't have a phone with me."

"Here, you can use mine."

She got her cell phone out and helped me dial the numbers. When I heard my mom's voice, my chest gripped with pain. I knew I needed to call Mom, but I hadn't taken time to think of what I was going say. I couldn't tell her that Dad was dead. No one had actually made that statement yet. I didn't want her to panic and be in a state of fear as I was, but I knew she needed to know it was serious. I don't remember what I said, but whatever it was, I knew my mom understood. When I got off the phone, the paramedic came over to me and asked if I wanted to get into the ambulance with him, because they were getting ready to leave for the hospital. The man's face was a haze to me, but I remember the sound of his voice. He was calm and gentle. His gestures were very kind, and I knew it was an attempt to comfort my raw emotions.

I sat in the ambulance, while I watched the men continue their attempt to resuscitate my Dad. For a brief moment, a thought came to me. "You can pray! Go pray for your dad. Pray to God to bring him back to you. No, demand that God restores him. After all God is able to do anything, even bring a man back from the dead." Then, at that very second, in a flash of time, I heard another voice, and this time it wasn't mine.

"Do you really want to do that? Dad's body was betraying him. He had pain here on earth that he had never had before. Today could be the beginning of the most glorious day of his life. Do you really want to stop him from seeing Me?"

I made a decision. I decided to leave my dad's life in the hands of God.

As we headed for the hospital, I knew things were not good. The ambulance took off very slowly. The drive was calm, and there were no sirens used to get him to the hospital. There was no rush to get him to the hospital. The man who sat next to me was calm and kind, and we drove in silence. There was nothing for him to say. I was praying that God would help me learn how to live this new life. My new reality was now one without my father.

Then it happened again. Darkness began to settle over my soul as this relentless vicious demon slithered onto the scene. This devil was getting more brazen and calculating. This wicked opportunist took this moment to charge in and deliver another brutal attack. As we were entering the parking lot of the hospital, I heard that cruel voice shouting in my ear, "YOU FAILED! You are such a failure. The one person who believed in you and knew that you could do anything is dead, and he never got to see you be victorious over your problems. You failed him, just like you will fail everyone in your life. You are pathetic, and your life will never be better than it is right now, at this moment. This is the darkness you will live in forever."

My whole body shook with the sound of the curses and the condemnations. A shiver rushed through my body, and I knew God was saying, "Put a stop to this." I shouted in my mind, "NO.........! I will not listen to this evil message. My father loved me and was proud of me. God loves me, and Jesus protects me. YOU HAVE TO LEAVE!" I was now protected, at least for that day. Things would never be the same again. It was the beginning of a new life. It was the beginning of a new venture.

CHAPTER 3

Where I End, God Begins

[11] For he shall give his angels charge over
thee, to keep thee in all thy ways.

[12] They shall bear thee up in their hands, lest thou
dash thy foot against a stone. Psalms 91:11-12

*"I have heard it said that if you take the number of angels
referenced in the bible and you divide them up by the number
of Christians on earth, each Christian would have something
around 20,000 angels a piece fighting on their behalf. I have
found comfort in this statement many times in my life"*

The sky was gloomy and gray, and there was a misty rain
that seemed to be so light and airy that it was as if the water
was suspended; floating as to make a continuously translucent
sheet of water. The road made a humming noise as the man
peddled his bike along the rain-covered path. In the seen world,
one could hear whispers coming out of the lips of the man as
he rode. If one was close enough to actually discern what he
was saying, they would hear that his utterings were words of
praise and a conversation with the truest friend this man had.

In the unseen world there was a great stirring. The legion of angels, the protectors and guardians of this man, began to look up in the sky. A great event was about to take place. The angels knew what was coming and they broke out into a heavenly chorus. Their song turned into songs of praise and majesty for a great happening was taking shape. A silver line appeared in the sky. A brilliant stream of light pierced the gloominess that consumed the expanse. Then the silver line became bigger as the sky began to open. The heavenly host escalated their joyous song as God's great messenger appeared on the scene. It was at this moment, the spiritual eyes of the man who was riding the bike on the side of the lonely road were open. He could see the glory that was all around him and he saw God's angel approach.

The host of angels too grew quiet as the Lord's messenger began to speak. "Dan, I have some good news for you."

Dan looked at the angel, "I love good news. What is it?"

The angel replied, "Dan, there is a party going on in heaven and Jesus, your dearest Lord and Master, is waiting for you to celebrate. This Party is for you. You have lived a faithful life here on earth, and it is time for you to come and live in Glory." At that moment this celestial being stretched his hand out toward Dan, and Dan took hold with anticipation. In a flash, Dan's spirit ascended toward God, and Dan's physical body was left lifeless in the ditch. It was a truly glorious day in heaven and the most tragic of days here on earth.

The day Dad went home to be with Jesus was a turning point in my life and a breaking point. Prior to Dad's death, I spent hours upon hours thinking of different ways that I could solve the problems of my life. I would make plans and act on them only to have them fail miserably. I would rely upon the "gifts" I knew God had given me in order to sort out all the deficiency I had. This system never brought victory. I spent sleepless nights not approaching God with my petty problems. They were small, insignificant problems that I could take care of with a little common sense. I would save my "Secret Weapon" for more life altering problems. After all, I had made my bed, so it was my responsibility to now sleep in this proverbial bed. The phrase "Pray like it is all up to God, but work like it is all up to me" became my motto. The thing is, "small" problems become very numerous and overwhelming. Soon they create great turmoil, as was in my case. No matter how hard I tried to help myself, I was never successful.

One night I was in utter agony. I could not sleep, so Jeff had picked up the Bible and was reading to me in an attempt to comfort me. I tried with all my might to settle down so I could sleep. His voice was soothing and calm, and I began to relax. Then I heard him read a sentence from the Bible that stunned me so completely that my eyes flew open. "Hope deferred makes the heart sick." I stiffened and moaned when I heard this phrase. I thought, "Are you kidding me! The Bible is even prophesying my present state of being." I deliberated some more. "Well for Pete's sake!!", I shouted in my mind. "What am I doing this for? Why am I trying so hard to live my life in God and put my hope in God if at the end of the day my heart is still sick?" I was so mad. No, by this point I was furious. I couldn't tell for sure who I was really livid with, myself or God, and that frightened me. One thing was for sure, I knew I had come to the end of myself. I seriously had no more to give. I even wondered if I should give up, but where would that take me? I didn't know what to do, and thankfully, somewhere inside of me I knew the answer was with God. I knew that right here and right now is the end of me, and it has to be the beginning of God.

***

A few days after Dad's introduction into heaven, I was up very early in the morning with my Bible in my lap. I hadn't really started reading yet, because I didn't really know what to read. I had spent so many years reading the Bible because it was the right thing to do, but now that didn't seem to be good enough.

I really needed to read the Bible to get some results in my life. I needed the Bible to save me and be my friend. I needed God's Word to comfort me and guide me. I didn't have a clue where to start. My heart was heavy and burdened, so I decided to read in Psalms. It seemed the natural place to go for comfort. I began to read when a soothing Spirit ran over my body. It felt good for me to know that I was in the presence of the Lord. Then I heard a voice speak to me. It was an inward impression that I knew was God. He said, "Leanne, I know your experiences with the enemy have been very painful. I want you to know that I have always been with you. I have

23

never left you. You have had some battles, and I was there with you when you were fighting them. However, there is one thing that Satan has said to you that is truth. "Your best will never be good enough." That is why I came. I have offered myself to be more than enough for you. It is time for you to learn that you do not have to impress me. I love you. And because Jesus' Spirit is in you, I am pleased. You do not have to try and help yourself out of these sticky situations. I have come to get you out of these sticky situations. You do not have to fight these battles on your own, just to prove something to me. I have come to fight the battles for you. Finally, you do not have to fight for Me or defend Me. I have already won everything that there is to win. I AM the great I AM, and I will do all of this for you if you let go of yourself and your own abilities and hand it all over to me. My job is to work. Your job is to trust and believe. You are my warrior and this is the Warrior Way. Let's begin a new journey together: one where I do all the work, and you learn how to believe and have faith."

The message I got from God was clear. It was the same message that I had been receiving for years and years. I was so busy trying to do the right thing, that I never really received it. There is a saying, "When the student is ready the teacher will appear." Ironically, in an instant, my divine teacher appeared.

One morning I was up earlier than usual, because I couldn't sleep. I was anxious, and I needed to hear the sound of voices, so I turned on the television. Since there wasn't anything worth watching, I ended up on a Christian Broadcast Station. Something caught my attention, and I paused on the channel long enough to hear the man say, "Today, we are going to talk about 'Faith, The Power to Bring the World to Its Knees'."

I wasn't sure I heard him correctly, so I continued to listen, just in case. Was this man getting ready to talk specifically about faith? I wondered and watched in skeptical curiosity. I have heard faith preached on before, but it always seemed to be something intangible and elusive. Faith always felt like something I was striving for but could never really attain. I wondered if this man would give me anything more than what I already knew. How many times had I heard the words, "Just have faith."? In the back of my mind, I would smile and say, "Yes, that is right. But how?" It was the, but how, that always got me. I knew the right things that I should do as a Christian. It was the execution that sometimes stumped me. I didn't always know "how" to have faith or "how" to believe or "how" to get the job done. I wondered, as I watched this man, if he would be able to communicate to me anything new. I wondered if he would be able to show me the "how" to my faith, so I watched. By the end of the morning I was in tearful joy. Not because all my problems were solved in one morning, but I could see that I was getting some answers.

This book is going to show you what some of those answers were for me. I will give you some skills and strategies to take into your life that will begin to help you learn how to fight the enemy and win every time. You are more than a conqueror through Christ who gives you strength. You have the ability to win every battle every time. This is a promise. This book is going to show you how. Are you ready? Let's Go!

CHAPTER 4

The Sword

"All God's promises are yes and amen." 2 Corinthians 1:20

A fundamental part of being a Christian is that one has to resolve the Bible is absolute truth. There comes a point, in every Christian's life, where just agreeing with the Bible is not enough. One must be totally assured that God's Word is the final authority and unconditional certainty. There is no room for doubt. We must learn to "Just Believe".

I remember very clearly the morning I got up and was reading my Bible out of desperation to find some answers to my problems. I came across the verse, "You can do all things through Christ who gives you strength." Philippians 4:13 I was in such a dark and doubtful place in my life that I said out loud, "I don't know if that is really true." The words that came out of my mouth shook me. I thought to myself, "What do you mean you don't know if this is true? I guess, Leanne, you are at a crossroad in your life. You're going to have to decide whether you believe the Bible or not. If you do decide you are going to believe in the Bible, you are going to have to believe the whole Bible." I sat there for a moment to give myself time to make this resolute decision in my heart. I weighed the question in my mind. Is the Bible true?

Scientists have proven the Bible as a legitimate historical piece of literature. History has shown that 100% of all the Old Testament prophecies have come to pass. Research reveals that in order for just 8 of those prophecies to come to pass, the odds would be 1 in 10,000,000,000,000,000,000,000,000,000. (A Case for Christ by Lee Strobel) There are over 300 prophecies in the Old Testament that have been fulfilled, which completely blows the mind to think of the probability of that happening. If you were a gambling man, you would be a fool not to bet on the Bible. With these types of statistics, you can be assured that the Bible is a sure thing. All of these discoveries have been key in strengthening my faith in God. The Word had transformed my life and my heart, and yet I still had to take a moment and ask myself, "Is the Bible really true?"

My heart screamed a resounding, "Yes! It is true." Just because I wasn't experiencing everything I wanted to experience, didn't mean the Bible wasn't true.

I made a decision that day to believe that the Bible was the indisputable Word of God. If my eyes did not see God and my mind did not understand His ways, I would still believe. The heavens were opened up to me that day. I began to see the majesty of God and His influence on this world in a way I had never seen before. The Bible became alive to me. God's promises became personal. I began to read the Bible as if God Himself had written this book just for me.

A few days later I read the verse. "I am more than a conqueror through Christ who gives me strength." Romans 8:37 I am <u>MORE</u> than a conqueror?! A conqueror is a person who overcomes his enemy and wins all his battles. A conqueror wins every battle, every time!! The bible says that you and I are MORE than a conqueror though Christ who gives us strength. Now as I said these words, knowing that they were there for me, I began to believe.

I began to quote this verse every morning as I was getting out of bed. It was as though I was dressing in armor before Satan would attack me. I would say these powerful words out loud to drown out any doubt or discouragement before the day even had begun. It worked. I found myself winning that one battle. I was becoming a conqueror.

"The word of God is living and active, sharper than any two-edged sword, piercing to the division of soul and of spirit, of joints and of marrow, and discerning the thoughts and intentions of the heart." ESV Hebrews 4:12 I didn't completely understand this passage, but one thing was certain, every Warrior needs a weapon. According to this scripture that weapon is the Bible. It is the sword that must become part of us in order to win every battle every time. Excitement filled my soul, and I acted upon the opportunity to get the Word of God into my soul. It was no longer a discipline, but it was something I desired. This Bible was now my sword.

I now will use this weapon to fight off the attacks of the enemy. Since the enemy is relentless and unwilling to ever back down from his ruthless attacks, I need to be very familiar with my weapon, for it is my sword! "This is my Bible. I have what it says I have. I am who it says I am. I can do what it says I can do. I am more than a conqueror through Christ who gives me strength. I am a warrior and this is the Warrior Way."

Note: You may have just picked up this book and started reading. As you are reading through, you know you are not a Christian. If that is the case, your first step is to believe Jesus is the Son of God, and He came and gave His life so that you can be saved. Receiving salvation is the first of all steps to having a victorious life on this earth and beyond.

Sin is an ugly thing. We all know how ugly it is, because we see the effects of it around us daily. Sin is as simple as missing the mark. And the imperfection of sin is so profound that the payment for sinning is death. From the beginning this fact broke God's heart, so He designed a way for man not to have to pay the price for sin. He sent His son, Jesus, who knew no sin, to be sin; to pay the price for us, so that we might be the righteousness of Christ and be saved. Through Jesus' sacrifice we are now able to live with God forever in eternity. REMEMBER, grace and salvation cannot be earned. It is given to us freely from God. You must, however, receive it and accept it. Pray this prayer with a genuine heart and you will be saved.

"God, thank you that you are a God that loves me. I recognize that I am a sinful person. I have missed the mark in many areas of my life and have failed. I am ready to ask you to forgive me of my sin and receive the salvation of Jesus Christ. I surrender my life to

you. I know I am unable to change my wicked ways, but I believe that you have the power to change me. Thank you for the sacrifice you paid on the cross so many years ago. Thank you for coming into my spirit and making me new. I pray this in Jesus name. Amen."

CHAPTER 5

Drawing Your Sword

"For the word of God is living and active, sharper than any two-edged sword, piercing to the division of soul and of spirit, of joints and of marrow, and discerning the thoughts and intentions of the heart." Hebrews 4:12

Why do so many Bibles sit on a shelf and collect dust? If the Bible holds all of the answers of the universe, then why are so many people unfamiliar with what is actually written inside on its pages? The answer is simple. There is a great advisory that hates God so much that he is willing to take that hatred out on you. He knows that the Bible shows the true nature of God and points the way to eternal victory. Because of this, Satan manipulates people in every way he can in order to prevent mankind from finding their answers in the Word of God. Satan knows the Bible is true, and he hates it!! If a person is willing or unknowingly neglecting their source of power, Satan will take advantage of that and he will attack and attack hard. He is relentless, and will never give up his pursuit to generate discouragement, fear and ultimate destruction. For this reason, this chapter is dedicated to the training of "how" to use your Bible as the Sword to fight off the enemy and win every time.

"The definition for insanity is doing the same thing over and over again and expecting different results." (Albert Einstein). Nothing changes until you make a change. The only difference between a rut and a grave is the depth of the hole. I have heard all of these statements many times, and have discovered them to be totally and completely true! Years I spent in the "What Zone", never managing to completely emerge into the "How Zone". Most of my life, pastor, teachers, leaders and friends who loved me would tell me what I needed to do to have spiritual success. How many times did I hear the words, "You need to pray about this situation?", "Don't forget to read your Bible, every day.", "Glean from God's wisdom.", "Walk in the Spirit.", "Be in the World but not of the World", and one of my favorites, "Let go and let God." At times, I would feel like pulling my hair and screaming in frustration, "YES, BUT HOW!" While all of the statements and comments are utterly correct, and I agree with them wholeheartedly, I spent a good majority of my life knowing "what" to do, but never fully understanding "how".

I need to pray, but how am I supposed to pray? Read the Bible, but how should I read the Bible? Live in God's wisdom. How do I live in God's wisdom, especially when I don't know what His wisdom is? Let go and let God? Really? The simplest of statements has the most difficult execution.

Much of my torment over the years was that I always knew what I was supposed to do, but I just never fully understood how to do it. Randomly turning the pages of the Bible, hoping that something would pop out at me, just wasn't cutting it when my battles became overwhelmingly real.

You may be feeling exactly as I was, and this next section is for you. Your heart is pounding in the same frustration. Being stuck in a rut is making you sick and tired, and you are sick and tired of being "sick and tired". You are done with letting Satan manipulate your mind and emotion. Maybe you are unhealthy and your body is shutting down, but you just can't stand the thought of giving up. Perhaps you are in lack of money, and the stress of the monthly bills weighs so heavily on you that you feel as if you can barely breathe. Possibly, you have a child that is ill. You want to pray and fight on their behalf, but you don't know what to say or how to pray. It could be that your children have turned their backs on their faith, and they are living in a destructive lifestyle. Maybe you're in a situation where you are being attacked at work by a co-worker or a boss. You might be the victim of vicious gossip, and you have undergone brutal character sabotage. There is the chance you personally are living in such a deep pit of sin and despair that you believe there is no way out. You are at the end of your rope, and you are holding on by a thread. One wrong move and you will lose completely. Life may be giving you multiple struggles all at once. You feel like your head is underwater and you are breathing through a straw. There is also the chance that you are living a peaceful and seemingly problem free life, but there is a constant nagging at your soul that something is missing. All of these reasons and thousands more are fantastic reasons to keep on reading.

Learning to draw your Sword is a three-step process. I recommend you get a journal to help you with this process. It can be a writing journal or a 3-ring binder with lined paper inside. It really doesn't matter what you use. You need something to write your thoughts down in, and then later a place to record your results.

Step 1: Before you begin anything, pray this prayer: "God, thank you for being a God that loves me. Thank you for always being there for me, even when I shut your voice out and I cannot feel your presence. My heart's desire is to know You more. I pray that You will open up my mind and soul to You and that You will give me Your Wisdom to take this next step in my healing process. I thank You that, no matter what I have done or where I am today, You love me. I praise You, because You have already fought all my battles for me and won. Now, I thank you for teaching me how to fight my own battles with Your strength. I give my battles to You. I fully surrender my life to You and Your care. Show me what to do to have full victory."

Congratulations! That is the first prayer of the rest of your life. The prayer you just prayed will help you get through the next step and eventually give you ultimate victory.

Step 2: On a piece of paper make a list of the struggles you are facing. Write as fast as you can, without thinking about it too much. Brainstorm this list. Write down every thought and frustration that comes to your mind. You could start out with simple issues and progress into deeper ones. This step can be emotionally draining and challenging. You need to pray before you start, while you are creating the list, and immediately afterwards. DO NOT dwell on this list for too long. This list is a starting point, not an ending point. This list is written down for the single intention of destroying it, NOT to live in it. Please remember that.

OK, let's go with God.

Example follows. You, however, should create your own list.

	Battle of my life
	1. I have no gas in my car
	2. My back hurts at night
	3. I don't have time to get groceries
	4. A mean co-worker
	5. No job advancement possible
	6. Overwhelming pressure at work
	7. Always fighting with my husband
	8. I have no friends
	9. I have no money
	10. No one loves me
	11. I am a bad parent

This list is for your eyes only. It is between you and God. You may share it ONLY with someone you trust. They are not allowed to be a "Drama Partner" or "Character Basher". They must be a "Prayer Warrior" whom you know will pray on your behalf. Do not share this list with someone who will pity you, or agree with all your problems. Also, do not share your list with someone who will use your struggles against you. Only share this list with someone who is willing to stand against your troubles and battle with the power of God. Simply share with people who believe God is more powerful than your troubles!!! That is a must.

Step two is designed to show you how much you need God. You cannot fight these battles and win all on your own. You need a Savior. And that Savior is Jesus and His Holy Spirit. When I created this list, it became a breaking point for me. I became fully aware that I was never going to be good enough or smart enough or wise enough to fix the problems in my life. I came to the end of myself. It was also the beginning of my realization that God was my only answer. This is the beginning of real change. You are daring to believe that you can step out of your rut and leave the grave behind. Right now is the next stage to making changes that will transform your life forever. Understanding your battles is the beginning to true victory. I want you to take some time right now to complete this exercise before going on to the next section.

*****Pause*****

Step 3: Very good. You did it. Now, what do you do with this notorious list of shortcomings and struggles? It is simple. Go to the Word. I said it was simple, not easy. This is going to be the most labor intensive part of drawing your Sword. You must go to the Word and find out what the Word has to say about your trouble and let the Word of God fight your battles.

For instance, let's say that you are dealing with unexplained and uncontrollable fear. Go to the Word. Look up scriptures that talk about fear. What does the Bible say? **Psalms 23:4** *"Yea, though I walk through the Valley of the shadow of death, I will fear no evil: For You are with me; Your rod and Your staff, they comfort me."* Or perhaps this one strikes a chord with you.

Psalms 91:5 *"I will not fear the arrow that flies by day or the pestilence that stalks in the darkness."* **Psalms 91:*11*** *"He will command His angels concerning you to guard you in all your ways. They will lift you up in their hands so you do not strike your foot against a stone."* Wow! Now isn't that comforting? Not only is it comforting, it's true. Do not try and argue with the Bible. Your job is to confess and believe. You have angels that are commanded to take care of you. Heavenly beings that get their orders from God Himself. Now that is empowering. There are dozens of more verses that battle this wickedness called fear.

Perhaps your struggle is with finances: not having enough or having an overwhelming debt. It eats away at you. Take a minute to see what the Bible says about provision or prosperity.

Philippians 4:19 *"And my God will supply every need of yours according to his riches in glory in Christ Jesus."* **2 Corinthians 9:8** *"And God is able to make all grace abound to you, so that having all sufficiency in all things at all times, you may abound in every good work."* **Psalms 37:25** *"I have never seen the righteous forsaken, nor their seed begging bread."* Know God is on the scene and He is going to make a way when you don't see any way. He said he would do this for you, and He is going to do this through the Spirit of Jesus Christ and for His Glory.

I personally use the website http://www.openbible.info/ to find the scriptures that help me. There are many ways to find scriptures that apply to your situation. You simply must take the time to search.

As you are looking up and reading your Sword. It is very important that you meditate on what you are reading. Look into the scripture with great intent. Ponder what you are reading and do not merely read over it quickly to get the job done. As you are reading, ask God to reveal his true message of the scripture. Seek for your spiritual eyes to be opened, so that God's power is revealed to you as you read. While you are taking this incredible journey of discovery, focus on taking the words that you are reading and turn them from, "I hope this is true," to "I agree that this is true for others," to "this is true for me." Ask God to help you in your unbelief.

When you are selecting your Swords (scriptures), I recommend that you take one battle at a time. Do not try and tackle everything all at once. Take the obstacle that seems to be the most crippling to you and begin your battle there. As you begin to grow stronger in your belief and emotions, you can take on the others a few at a time. God is patient. He loves you. He is not angry with you, and you do not live under a curse for anything you have done or might not have done. Jesus took the curse for you, on the cross, over 2000 years ago, so that you might live in God's blessing. Be at peace while you learn to fight these battles. Remember, God has already fought these battles and won. The real battle is the one raging in you. Today you took the first steps to winning your battles and having complete victory over the enemy.

NOTE: When you are looking up scripture to help you through a certain situation, make sure you read all the verses before and after your power scripture. Be careful to always use your scriptures in the context that they were intended. Taking scripture out of context and bending it to support your own desired interpretation is a dangerous thing to do. If you are uncertain as to the meaning of a passage of scripture, seek out trusted counseling or just keep on reading. Let the Bible explain itself. The Bible will never contradict itself and will always interpret itself! Seek and you will find.

CHAPTER 6

Swinging Your Sword

"The armies of heaven were following him, riding
on white horses and dressed in fine linen, white and
clean. Coming out of his mouth is a sharp sword with
which to strike down the nations." Revelation 19:14-15

Warrior was posed in the center of the battlefield. A great conflict was raging all around him. He maintained keen observation of his surroundings as he surveyed the state of affairs in order to determine the next strategic move. In an instant, one of his grueling adversaries was charging toward him. The creature had gray leathery skin, and his yellow teeth were dripping saliva as he screeched out his evil battle cry. With a spear in his hand, he was preparing to run his weapon directly through Mighty Warrior's heart. When all at once, Mighty Warrior drew his Sword so quickly that it moved the air, and all one could see was a flash of light. The demon's spear clashed against Warrior's Sword with such great force it made the ground shake underfoot. This monster stalled for a moment as if shocked at his thwarted attempt to penetrate the heart of this man. He lifted his spear up to make another attempt at his heart. Warrior easily batted away the devil's spear with his Sword once again. It was obvious that Warrior was very familiar with his Sword. It was as if it was an extension of his body. In fact, it was hard to see where Warrior ended and his Sword began. Warrior was fearless as he stood his ground, ready to fight the minions of Satan. At that moment, the spear of the great oppressor clashed once again into the Sword. Warrior stood with confidence and strength, while the enemy frantically lashed out. This grim and evil opposition was striking at Warrior from every angle and from every direction. Every time this villain would come down on Warrior he was prepared, and he used his Sword to protect himself from the blows. Then instantaneously, Warrior had decided that this battle had gone on long enough. He outstretched His Sword high above his head, and with one mighty swing he slashed right through the belly of his enemy. In an instant the aggressor was gone. Warrior was victorious, and the battle was won.

I don't know much about fist fighting, hand to hand combat, or even boxing, but I do know it takes a huge amount of preparation to get ready for a fight. Frankly the thought of getting into a ring with a person, whose sole purpose is to beat the snot out of me, frightens me. However, it is a perfect scenario showing the battle we face with Satan daily. Let's take a look for just a moment. There are two fighters ready to battle it out. One comes in with years of training. He has hours in the gym lifting unknown amounts of weights, and he has immeasurable amounts of time in the ring practicing for the next big fight. This man has practiced all the moves and all the tricks of the trade. He knows jabs, right hooks, upper cuts and more. He has spent much time in the ring observing his opponents and their behavior. He knows just how to wear his rival down. Then the moment for which he has been waiting happens. His opponent's facial expression is that of one just before they are ready to give up: the expression of exhaustion and despair. It is in that moment when an experienced boxer goes in for the knock out. BAM!! He has won.

In contrast, there is the man who doesn't even know he is in a fight and yet finds himself in the middle of the ring, crowds chanting, adrenaline racing, and people waiting with anxious anticipation to see who will emerge the champion. This second man is totally unprepared and untrained. He has only been in a gym and has never actually used any of the equipment. He has never thrown a punch before, nor has he ever had physical contact in his life. Who do you think is going to dominate this conflict?

It is easy to see who will most likely be the victor in this situation. This is exactly what happens to Christians when they are not prepared to battle Satan. "Satan is like a roaring lion seeking whom he may devour." *1 Peter 5:8* Satan has years and years of practice, millenniums to be precise. He knows just which buttons to push. He has observed you from infancy. He knows what gets you angry and frustrated. He sees the situations that cause great fear. He watches your face and antics like a hawk in order to know what it takes to cause you to doubt and to stumble. He takes the time to discover your areas of temptation. He gets a sense of pride when he is able to throw temptation into your path. He ascertains your greatest pain and sorrow, and when you are not paying attention, he will hit you where it hurts most, over and over again. He will never stop, and he never takes a day off. It is for certain that Satan will always attack in areas he perceives as weakness. His victims will always be the people who are unprepared.

It is a mystery to me why anyone would enter into a cosmic battle with a foreboding enemy and not prepare themselves for the fight! For years, even as a Christian, I did not recognize there was such a great battle. I thought I must be down on my luck or that my trouble was "just the way things are." You may feel the same way. All I have to say is, NO!!! This is absolutely not the truth. Trouble in your life is the desire of the devil. "Our battle is not against flesh and blood, but against principalities and rulers of this dark world." *Ephesians 6:12* God's plan is that you reign victorious and that you win all your battles. Your troubles are an attack of Satan and your training field for God. God wants you to learn how to fight using the unbeatable weapons that he has so graciously given you. The Holy Spirit and God's Word!! God wants you to stand and take authority. "All authority in heaven and on earth has been given to you." *Matthew 28:18* You have the power to win, and God wants you to win.

Your victories will greatly depend upon how well you know your Weapon. If you own a Bible that sits on the shelf and you never touch it, you are not prepared to fight the enemy. He will attack you, and he will win. He cannot take your salvation, but he will take your peace and steal your life. Perhaps you do read the Bible but only because it is the proper thing to do. If so, you are not seeking nor searching ways to know your God better or to discover the tactics to fight your enemy. The devil is not going to "take it easy" on you just because you are not prepared. He doesn't work that way. He is an opportunist, and he has absolutely NO grace and NO mercy to give. He will come at you with both guns blazing and he will not stop until he has won

In the last chapter I explained to you what it means to "draw your Sword." That is the first step in the rules of engagement. However, can you imagine how ridiculous Warrior would look if he went into this great cosmic battle with his "all powerful" Sword, and he never swung it? Imagine watching that on a movie screen. A great and mighty warrior comes on the scene to fight in a celestial battle. Everyone knows he is the hero, and they wait with baited breath ready to see a mighty battle and a great victory. The warrior takes his place front and center in the war zone and draws his sword with confidence. Then…. just stands there…. and he keeps standing there until he is struck down and has lost. That seems ridiculous. Everyone would laugh their way out of the movie theater, and the level of disappointment would be overwhelming. People would leave saying, "That was the stupidest movie I have ever seen." It would be a box office disaster. Just as it will be a disaster for you if you draw your Sword and never swing it.

Drawing your Sword is your defense against your enemy. Swinging your Sword is your offensive. "… *if you confess with your mouth that Jesus is Lord and*

> *believe in your heart that God raised him from the*
> *dead, you will be saved." Romans 10:9 ESV*

Confession is the next step you must take in order to win every battle every time. That is right! I said confession. Speaking it out loud. Saying what the bible says is truth. Using the Word of God to fight off every attack the enemy sends your way. While drawing your sword is the most labor intensive part of your training, confessing the Word of God is going to take the most courage.

It is essential that you say God's promises out loud for everyone to hear. It is most important for you to hear your confessions. Your body and your mind believe what your mouth says. Your body actually responds at a cellular level to the sound of your voice. The best mode to change a way of thinking is to hear the confession of your own mouth.

God is in your heart, and He knows your every thought. Satan, on the other hand, cannot read your thoughts. He can only interpret your expressions and hear the words that come from your mouth. If he sees your body language speaking stress and anxiety and then the words that come out of your mouth support his assumption, he knows he is winning. However, when you turn the table on him and you choose to speak the Words of God, Satan is defeated.

When you speak the Word of God out loud, you paralyze and neutralize the enemy. He cannot fight against the Word of God. He may try to trick you into believing that he can, but the real truth is he has NO power against the Word of God. That is why every time you choose to take God's Word into your heart and confess it with your mouth, Satan has to flee. He loses.

The scriptures you choose to fight your battles with are your Swords. Take them out and use them regularly. Draw your Sword against Satan daily and begin to watch God win. When Satan comes down on you with things like, "You are such a loser. You are never going to make it through this impossible situation," you can come back to him, full voice, with "No! God says that I am more than a conqueror through Christ who gives me strength." *Romans 8:37*

Satan continues, "Oh yeah? That is what you think? What about the fact that you have absolutely no money in the bank and all your bills are due next week. What are you going to do then? You are probably going to be put out of your house."

Your rebuttal is, "God has promised to protect me and to prosper me. 'He has given me all sufficiency in all things always.' (*2 Corinthians 9:8*) I don't know how God is going take care of me; I just know that He is."

Satan's relentless reply is, "Why in the world would you think God is going to come in and save you? Don't you remember all the mistakes you have made? You are a dirty rotten sinner and you are ugly. You have the disgust of sin written all over you." You retort, "God loves me so much that he sent Jesus to die for all my sins. Because I believe in Jesus I am saved, and God loves me as if I were the only person in the world to love. *(John 3:16)* I am the righteousness of Christ. *(2 Corinthians 5:21)* I know that He is going to take care of me, AND in Jesus name you have to leave me alone. Be gone with you!" *John 3:16, Luke 10:17.* Hallelujah. You win!

I want to remind you that this whole interaction seems to be a one-way conversation. Satan's battlefield is in your mind, silent to the world around you. Your offensive move is in your spoken confession, saying it out loud. You are going to feel ridiculous and crazy but don't stop. That is exactly how Satan wants you to feel. He does not want you to battle him with a weapon he knows is going to defeat him. It doesn't matter how you feel. Stand firm and do it anyway. If someone happens to hear you during one of your battles, they may think you are schizophrenic. It doesn't matter. Get yourself into a private area and keep on battling until you win.

A great place to practice this is in the privacy of your home. Start your warrior training in the morning so you can perform in its power all day long. Find the scriptures that most fit the trials that may face you during the day and begin to confess them out loud. You can sit in your favorite chair with a cup of coffee and your Bible, or you may take a walk outside with your Bible. Either way make your confessions out loud for all the world to hear. It doesn't matter where you begin your practice, just begin. You need to become familiar with the sound of your own voice when it comes to fighting these battles. Quote scriptures over and over again until they automatically come into your mind at a moment's notice. Be familiar with the promises of God. Make them such a part of your life that it is as if they are written on the back of your hand. Then one day you will not only fight and win your battles, you will be empowered to help others fight their battles as well. That is a truly victorious day.

I must give you a couple of cautions. When you speak the Word of God over your life and your situation, you will run into a few obstacles. The first one is your personal lack of belief. When you say, "God has given me all sufficiency in all things all the time," (*2 Corinthians 9:8*) the first voice that stands in opposition to this statement may be your own. This will happen especially if you are living from paycheck to paycheck, and they are getting ready to turn off your electricity. You want to laugh out loud and say, "Well, that is not what it looks like in my life. It looks more like my life is going down the drain so fast that I can't stop it, and I am afraid to breath."

I am telling you that is exactly what the enemy wants you to think. "As a man thinks, so is he." (*Proverbs 23:7*) Your best response when bad news comes, is to say, "It may look like I am broke and without any hope, BUT, God says that He has given me all sufficiency in all things all the time. I do not know how I am going to get the money for this electric bill, but I know God is on the scene, and He is working on my behalf. God has a plan to prosper me and not to harm me. I live in all of God's goodness and today is the day that the Lord has made. I will rejoice and be glad in it." *(Jeremiah 29:11, Psalms 23:6, Psalms 118:24)* Say it out loud, over and over again and do not stop! Be as relentless as the enemy. Saying these words in the face of adversity takes courage and is key to complete victory.

Listen to what I am saying. When the devil attacks you in your mind, the only thing that will stop him in his tracks is your VERBAL confession. He is a master at mind games. He has had centuries to practice on all sorts of people from all around the world. If you try to battle Satan in your mind, you are going to lose that battle. Your train of thought is halted by your verbal profession of any sort, and that is what will stop Satan in his tracks. His realm is unseen and his battleground is in the mind. You level him down to naught when you verbally fight him with the Word of God. Satan hates the name, Jesus, and he cannot stand under the attacks of the Bible. He is subservient to God. God's Word reigns over ALL of his schemes.

The next point of opposition you will face when you practice verbal confession is the doubts and taunting of others. People around you will think you are strange. They will treat you like you are crazy. It is understandable when people in the world give you looks of confusion. It is a whole other ballgame when Christians look at you in disapproval and disbelief. When that happens, you must immediately release their attitudes and words to God. This is a place of surrender. God's plan and His purpose is more important than what people think. Their journey is "their journey". You must not stand in judgment of anyone, but at the same time you cannot let someone's lack of approval or disbelief stop you from doing what is right.

Your battles do not have to be public. Public fighting can cause confusion. For some people it may generate a great deal of fear streaming from a lack of understanding. You must be sensitive to people around you and let them make their own discoveries as God leads them. However, do not let your guard down. If Satan is attacking you in the middle of a grocery store, whisper your confessions out loud. A whisper is as effective as a shout when you are in the middle of a grocery store.

There also may be times when God is directing you to share what you know with someone who is ready and waiting to hear it. This is called being "led by the Spirit". It is that inner voice that says, "She needs your help, or he wants some answers. Tell him what you have learned." When you hear these inward impressions, do not be afraid. Be sensitive to the Holy Spirit and do as he instructs you, but that is a training for another day.

In conclusion, swinging your sword is a daily practice and a daily discipline. The more you are in the word and practicing your daily confessions the more prepared you will be when the time comes to actually fight the enemy. Start your practicing in a safe environment and do not be afraid to take the skill with you throughout the day. You will find yourself reigning victorious when night comes and you did not let your guard down, and you will see that out of your mouth comes a double edged Sword!!

Remember in all of your confessions, never forget to say, "'I can do all things through Christ who gives me strength.' *Philippians 4:13* God win's and because God wins I win"

For the word of God is living and active, sharper than any two-edged sword, piercing to the division of soul and of spirit, of joints and of marrow, and discerning the thoughts and intentions of the heart. Hebrews 4:12

CHAPTER 7

Living in the Sword

God and Man: God in Man

"Now may the God of peace himself sanctify you completely, and may your whole spirit and soul and body be kept blameless at the coming of our Lord Jesus Christ."
<u>1 Thessalonians 5:23</u>

Spirit, soul, and body. Every religion on earth talks about the spirit, soul, and body. The terms seem simple enough to understand, but if I ask you, right now, to give me your definition of spirit, what would you say? How about the term soul, what is a soul? Body seems simple enough to understand, but then there are times that you may wonder what, really, is this physical body for? And aren't the spirit and the soul the same thing? And if they aren't the same thing, then what is the difference between the two? Does it really matter if there is a difference?

The Bible says God sanctifies the spirit, soul and body and keeps them blameless. That is a very bold statement that many struggle with. It is very difficult in our human experience to find a blameless man. So why would the Bible make such a claim, and how can the Bible support this claim?

Understanding these terms better will give more of an understanding as to what the Bible is talking about in this scripture. *I Thessalonians 5:23* Understanding brings breakthrough. Check out this chart:

spirit ═══ soul ═══ physical body

To start off, man is a triune being. Man is a spirit, who has a soul and lives in a physical body. Man's spirit is the part that is uniquely him. It is his personality, his individualism, his true identity, so to speak. In the beginning when the Spirit of God created man, he made man out of mud and then breathed His breath into man and it brought life to him. God breathed into you your spirit. Your spirit is what gives you life in this physical world and, it is your spirit that will continue to live forever, long after this earthly life is over.

Next, man has a soul. Your soul is your mind, your will and your emotions. This is your thinker, your chooser and your feeler. Your soul is the part of you that thinks, contemplates, meditates and deliberates. Your soul is also the decision maker, the rudder that navigates the ship, so to speak. It is the part of you that makes those judgment calls and ultimately determines your course of action. Your soul is also the generator of all your emotions and your feelings. It determines your state of mind, your moods and your outlook on life. The soul is a very powerful part of your existence since you are a sum total of all the choices you make. A thought comes to you, which generates an emotion that ends in a choice, leading you down a course of action. Your life is a reflection of the choices you make. How your soul perceives life's situations is going to change your choices. If all of your thoughts tend to generate an emotion of fear, you will be making decisions that are fear driven. This is a very dangerous and limiting place to live. You create a very small comfort zone in which you can survive in, but you are unable to create an environment for thriving. However, the contrast is true as well. When you make your selections in life based out of adventure and empowerment, your world is opened up to endless possibilities. Two people can live in the same world with the same circumstances and have completely different outcomes in their lives. These outcomes can be solely based on the choices they have made, derived by the emotions they have allowed themselves to have. The fact of the matter is your soul ultimately determines how you will approach life. Respecting this high level of influence over you, it is very important to keep the soul in check and to monitor its activity. The best way to do this is to quit looking to your emotions alone to guide you.

Your emotions are what provide for your human experience. They bring you delight and a thrill, sorrow and sadness, hope and joy, and then one day you wake up and you're in the pit of despair. Emotions cannot always be trusted nor can they be ignored, and they should never completely control you. Emotions are highly volatile. When making your choices, you should use something more constant and stable as your guide. God is the only thing I know that is a true constant.

Therefore, He should continuously be your guide. Fortunately, His wisdom, usually, isn't any further than the bookshelf in your home. The Bible is packed full of God's wisdom, and His Holy Spirit is the inner voice that confirms the direction you should take. When your actions are driven by the Wisdom of God, you begin to live in the Will of God. The picture of your life begins to take a new shape.

The final portion of man is his physical body. You are composed of flesh and blood and bones. This body of yours is your vehicle that gets you from here to there. Your body is the part of you that lives and breathes and functions in this physical world. The activities your body engages in will be determined by your soul. Your body can live in and be subservient to this physical world. As a result, you become worldly. In contrast, you can choose to live a life following The Spirit of God and become Godly. The choice is yours.

I am not certain why you chose to start reading this book. There could be a dozen different reasons ranging from curiosity to complete and total desperation. Maybe somebody told you it was a good book. It doesn't really matter to me why you are reading. I just know that there is a reason you have this book in your hand at this moment. For it is at this moment that God wants you to begin to understand the overwhelming power of His Spirit and how to live in Him. This is the most valuable lesson anyone can learn and your learning starts right now.

Let's review for just a moment. As I stated earlier, drawing your Sword is the most labor intensive part of your fighting.

While swinging your Sword, your verbal confessions, takes the most courage, living in the Sword requires the most discipline and complete surrender. Living in the Sword is living in The Holy Spirit. The Sword is all God's promises that you read in His Bible. The Sword is the living Word of God. "In the beginning was the Word, and the Word was with God, and the Word was God." *John 1:1.* That is why it is so vitally important that you learn how to read and understand God's Word, for it shows you God. It must be a daily discipline to be in the Word in order to win all your battles all the time. Satan will continue to pursue you, therefore you must never stop pursuing an intimate relationship with God!

To understand this whole concept of "life in the Spirit" better, you must examine who the Holy Spirit really is and what He possesses. First, the Holy Spirit is the actual and literal Spirit of God. He is the personality of God, the character of God and the power of God.

What does the Holy Spirit possess? Well, my Bible says that He has all authority in heaven and on earth. *Matthew* 28:18 That means He possesses all love, all peace, all patience all wisdom, all kindness, all protection, all faith and all provision. God's Spirit lacks nothing! He is all sufficient in all things, always. That is powerful!

God's Word tells us that the Spirit will make His temple in the heart of man. 1 *Corinthians 3:16-17* Interesting statement, but what does that mean? Essentially man's heart, in this reference, is not his beating heart, but man's spirit. Now, reread that passage replacing the word heart with spirit. "God's Spirit will make His dwelling place in the spirit of man." If the Spirit of God, who lacks nothing, has made His dwelling place in the spirit of man, it stands to reason that there is an Almighty Power now in the spirit of a born again man that lacks nothing. This explains the scripture *in 2 Corinthians 9:8* "God is able to make all grace abound to you, so that having all sufficiency in all things at all times, you may abound in every good work." God is imparting His Spirit of sufficiency to you.

Only when you commit to a relationship, receiving His Spirit, will you be able to live in His power. He will reward those who earnestly seek him. *Hebrews 11:6*

God's rewards are not of this world. While they can show up through a physical manifestation in this world, the true rewards of God are intrinsic and eternal. The rewards of God originate in the spirit of man and then show up in the physical world around him. Through the renewing of your mind, God begins to teach you how to think the way He thinks and do as He would do. And then there are those moments when there is no earthly explanation for an outstanding blessing on your life. There is a moment when the impossible is all of a sudden made possible. It is in those moments that God receives all the glory through your life. God's reward is who He is. When you believe Him and seek Him, you will know Him better. His powerful attributes will begin to dominate your life. The day you asked God to be your Savior was the day He gave you ALL of His Holy Spirit. He did not come in part way. He came in all the way. All of God is in all of you, at least all of your spirit.

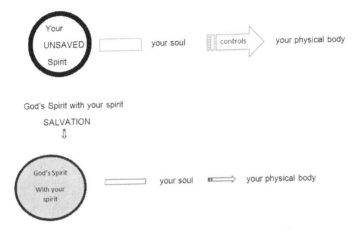

The benefits of God have been in you all along, since the day you were saved. However, you need to seek Him to unlock the mysteries of how to live in Him and have his attributes released in your life.

God is love. God does not have love to give. God is actually love. I mean God=Love. Now that true and pure love lives inside of you. When you seek God, you learn how to have and give that kind of love. It is a supernatural love that allows you to truly "love your enemies" and then go a step further and genuinely "bless those who curse you, and pray for those who spitefully use you" *Luke 6:28*

God is faithful. God does not have faith. He is faith. God=Faith. When we seek Him with all our hearts, His faith is released in our lives. So here is how it works. When God asks you to have faith for a situation in your life, and you begin to seek him and are looking to Him, you now tap into God's

Spirit of faith. That is the exact faith you need to get the job done. *James 12:2* WOW! Now if that is not a reward, I do not know what is. God literally rewards you with the manifestation of His character. All of God is already in you, now you get to learn how to live in all of what God has to offer. You will learn to live in all of God's love. That can transform your very character. You now learn to live in ALL of God's wisdom. This will alter all of your decision making abilities. Your choices will now take you down a new path, because you are making the choices God wants you to make. He teaches you and empowers you to live debt-free. He teaches you how to live so you have more than enough to give to every good work. He will reveal "good" ideas to you and block you from pursuing the "bad" ideas. All these physical benefits come from the reward of living in all of God's wisdom. You now can live in all of God's power. He will empower you to "get the job done", whatever the "job" is. The character attributes of God go on and on. You can see how learning how to live in God's Spirit will transform your life forever.

This untapped power is just sitting at your finger tips, and on the tip of your tongue. You tap into it simply by where you put your attention. The degree you live in the Holy Spirit will be determined by what your soul is focused on. Remember your soul? Your thinker, feeler, chooser. Well, your soul is the rudder of your ship. Man makes decisions based on emotions that are brought on by a thought. Many of your thoughts come to you through what you are looking at and what you are listening to. It is called our "Eye Gate", "Ear Gate" and "Mouth Gate". These are the "gates" in which you allow the outside world directly into your soul. If you are looking at negative material, often time you will think and contemplate the negative. If you are seeing or listening to positive material, your mind will be focused on the positive aspects of your life. What you give your attention to is the direction your life will go. When you pay attention to your career, your life action will be focused around your career and what it takes to improve your position. If your focus is on your family, your life will circle around your family. If you are focused on health, you will do all you can to become healthy. If you are focused on all the trouble you have coming to you, your life will evolve around your trouble. If you focus on the blessings that come to you, your life will be filled with blessings. What you focus on wins! Now take a look at how that effects the life you live with the Holy Spirit. "As a man thinks in his heart, so is he." *Proverbs 27:7* Look at the chart below:

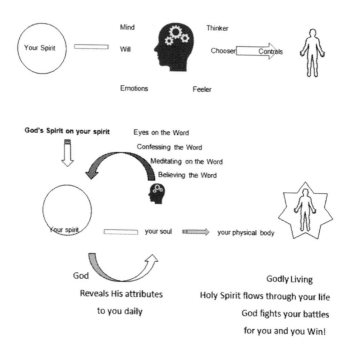

Galatians 5:16-17 "¹⁶ But I say, walk by the Spirit, and you will not gratify the desires of the flesh. ¹⁷ For the desires of the flesh are against the Spirit, and the desires of the Spirit are against the flesh, for these are opposed to each other, to keep you from doing the things you want to do."

Walking in the Spirit is a purposeful choice that you make by putting your eyes and your ears on the things of the Spirit. Your first and most important focus will be on God's Word. It is alive and active. If you don't know what to read, start by researching and reading your ever powerful Swords. Your Swords are all of God's promises. We now know that all of God's promises are "yes" and "amen". This is a great place to start. It opens up your "Eye Gate" to the mind of God. Then you begin to confess God's promises out loud. This, now, activates two more gates, your "Mouth Gate" by speaking and your "Ear Gate" by hearing the Word of God. Through these two activities, all three "Gates" are now fully aware of the Holy Spirit. This is a big step toward walking in the Spirit.

Once you start to make a personal relationship with your Bible, Words of God, you now are ready to take this commitment further into other areas of your life. Begin to listen to pastors and people that can guide you in the right direction. It is important to always filter what people say through the Word of God. It is challenging and exciting to take what you have heard and place it over the top of the Word of God. If it lines up with the Word of God, and it speaks truth to you, embrace it and thank God for the epiphany. However, if you filter it through the Word of God, and it doesn't match and there is inconsistency, you must throw it out and do not give any more of your time to it. Satan comes in to deceive and confuse, and one of his biggest weapons is conflicting information. The best lie is masked with an element of truth. And now because you are getting familiar with your Sword (Bible), you will be able to detect a lie when you see it.

The "I didn't know" argument is not going to mean anything when you find yourself in the middle of a mess. In fact, that is one of Satan's favorite phrases. He loves it when "you don't know". That is when he can take the most advantage of you. He also loves it when you separate your physical life from your spiritual life. As you begin this journey of a warrior

Leanne McDougall

and begin to put your eyes on the Word of God and make your confession, you also need to learn to guard your gates. What are you watching? Is the material you are allowing to go into your gates glorifying your God and bringing you into a closeness with Him, or is it material that is taking your soul in the opposite direction? The Bible calls this the direction of the flesh. When you shift your focus, you shift your walk. Satan wants you to believe that the entertainment and pleasure part of your life has nothing to do with your spiritual life. That is one more of his incredibly deceptive lies. Your soul has the responsibility to take your whole life in the direction of God. Look to God in the mornings when you are doing devotions, and all day long. Look to Him when you are listening to music, watching TV, talking with a friend and thinking about your plan for starting the next day. A life lived in Christ is one that spends the whole day making sure your mind stays focused in one direction. That is not to say that we will be thinking of the sovereignty of God all day long. It just means when you are at work and an opportunity to cuss your co-worker arises, you keep yourself in check. You keep your mouth shut, or better yet, you find a word of blessing instead. Gossip in the breakroom can be such a savory thing, however, we all know the destructiveness of gossip. At the moment of temptation, God reminds you that the person you are about to slander is one of His children too, and you should walk away. The entertainment of TV is many times relaxing and a way to decompress. When something shameful shows itself on the screen, you have the conviction to turn the channel or just turn the TV off altogether. When you neglect making an

64

appropriate choice, you have a "still small voice" in you that says, "Do the right thing. Do what I would do." That is the Holy Spirit talking to you, and it is your turn to listen. Thus you begin to be "led" by the Holy Spirit.

If you are unsure as to what types of things you should focus on to align yourself with the Holy Spirit, the Bible is very clear on that. "But **the** fruit **of the Spirit** is love, joy, peace, patience, kindness, goodness, faithfulness, gentleness, self-control; against such things **the**re is no law." *Galatians 5:22-23* The Bible is referring to these as fruits when they are manifested through your life. What they really are, are character traits of God flowing through you. If what you are allowing to enter into your gates support these characteristics that emulate God, then go for it.

However, the opposite is true as well. You must recognize the flesh and guard yourself from the worldly thinking. [17] "For the desires of the flesh are against the Spirit, and the desires of the Spirit are against the flesh, for these are opposed to each other, to keep you from doing the things you want to do. [18] But if you are led by the Spirit, you are not under the law. [19] Now the works of the flesh are evident: sexual immorality, impurity, sensuality, [20] idolatry, sorcery, enmity, strife, jealousy, fits of anger, rivalries, dissensions, divisions, [21] envy,[d] drunkenness, orgies, and things like these. I warn you, as I warned you before, that those who do such things will not inherit the kingdom of God." *Galatians 5: 17-21* Focusing on the flesh is a sure recipe for defeat in this world. Satan will not overtake your spirit, but he will capture your soul.

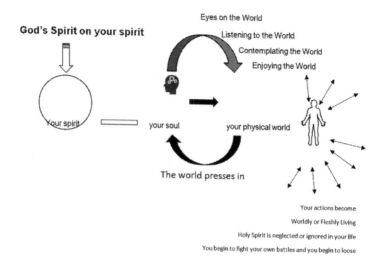

The Holy Spirit isn't lost in your life, but you will begin to loose battles. So guard what you watch, guard what you say, guard what you listen to, and guard what types of people you spend all of your time with. God will be there to help you and guide you all the way. Just watch, you will be following Jesus and opening yourself up to his guidance, and while watching your favorite TV show, you will get an inward impression. "That show is not truth. In fact, the material coming from their message is a total lie. I'm not going to watch that anymore." That is what we call living by the Spirit. It is the Spirit that made you aware of the wickedness that was coming from the TV. When these inward impressions come, your job is not to ignore them. Your job is to act in the way God is directing you to act. That is called your good works. Your "good works" is simply doing what the Lord tells you to do. Isn't that great?

Doesn't that take a lot of pressure off you? You don't have to constantly be wondering what you should do or how you should do it. You just continuously seek God, and He will reveal to you all that you should do. This is a life lived in the Holy Spirit and this is "The Warrior Way."

Chapter 8

Organizing Your Weapons

"Tabbing Your Bible"

"But in your hearts revere Christ as Lord. Always be prepared to give an answer to everyone who asks you to give the reason for the hope that you have. But do this with gentleness and respect." 1 Peter 3:15

Teenagers. Just the word sends a flood of emotions racing through most people's minds. Everyone has some type of opinion, one way or another, about teenagers or being a teenager. The general consensus is; if you are not quite a teenager yet, you can't wait to be one. If you are a teenager, you think you have arrived to the perfect state of coolness, or you are totally ready to not be a teen anymore. Adults are most often grateful when this precarious part of life is over. Then, they spend a good portion of adulthood praying that God will give them grace, mercy and wisdom to help their own children navigate their way successfully through that stage of life. It is a high level of intensity. In fact, during teenage years character is solidified or broken. For this reason, it is so important to stay as close as possible to your God during this time of your life. The choices a person makes during their teenage years are choices that can stay with them forever. It is important for all of us to choose wisely and to live in the privilege of God's grace and mercy. This choice will strengthen our character throughout our lifetime.

Being a teenage Christian can be a very powerful asset. Coming through the teen years with Jesus can build a person's faith in a way that nothing else can. Most people agree that teens can be relentless. They are bold and brazen and can, at times, be out-and-out cruel. Teens, many times, have a feeling that everyone should think and feel as they do. Any disagreement with a person brings the threat of being ostracized, called out and or challenged in their way of thinking or life choices.

Such was the case for me when I was in junior high and high school. When I was a child growing up in the church, no one questioned my church attendance or my faith. I thought that everyone believed as I did. After all, why wouldn't they want to believe in Jesus? He was the kindest person I knew, and we were always told of His Love and care for us. I thought the idea of Jesus was wonderful, and I thought that was what everyone else believed as well.

When I arrived in 7th grade of junior high, my eyes were opened. I quickly found out that very few people believed as I did, and I was immediately taunted and teased for being a Christian. I began to be questioned cruelly by my peers as to why I would believe in something as ridiculous as God or even Jesus. It was truly as though I was being spiritually kicked in the stomach and left breathless. When I was asked, "Why do you believe in Jesus?", I would reply with the most profound answer I could think of at the age of 13. "Because!"

Wow! Not only did that answer leave me feeling and looking stupid, and I'm sure I looked as dumb as I felt. I was empty inside as I thought to myself, "That is a really lame answer, Leanne, and you know it!" I decided right away that I needed to do something about the answer I had for my faith. The pressure and persecution was becoming great at school, and I found I had a choice to make. I could pretend like I wasn't a Christian and go along with the kids at school. That would enable me to live a seemingly peaceful life and perhaps even be considered "cool", or I could continue to profess my Christianity and become a social outcast. The idea of turning my back on my God and my parents was such a horrific and terrifying thought, I chose to be a social outcast.

Let's just say, I can't remember anything good about my early years in junior high school. I would get up most mornings and feel my stomach turn with anxiety, knowing I was going to the battle zone. Some classes were worse than others. I had no friends to look for when I entered the building or to ally with during the day. I was alone most of the time. A good class was one where everyone would just leave me alone and ignore me. The harder classes I spent the whole time trying to ignore all the taunts and teasing and threats.

I managed to be a shadow for most of my 7th and 8th grade years, but one day a young girl, who was angry with me and my religion, threatened to kill me. To this day, I don't know if she was serious or not, but I thought she was.

From the top of my lungs I began to yell in the girl's locker room following PE class. It was as if I had shattered, and I was not going to go down without a fight. I yelled for everyone to hear, "I have done nothing for you to treat me this way! Get away from me. You will not kill me, and you will not treat me like this anymore! I love God, and that is a good thing not a bad thing! Jesus is here with me! I will not be killed! I am going to live, and you are not going to kill me!" I slammed a locker door shut. I screamed even louder, "Leave me alone!!! Leave me alone!!! Leave me alone!!!" I was so scared I didn't know what else to say. I was crying out loud by the time the teacher appeared on the scene. Everyone in the locker room was watching and filled with total shock. They knew exactly what the situation was with me, and they did not expect for me to choose the toughest girl in school to make my first stand and debut my bravery. Most of the girls standing around had nothing to say. I do, however, remember a couple of girls show compassion toward me that day. It was the first indication of tenderness that I had received for nearly a year.

After that day, I am not sure if anyone really liked me better or not. Most of the key girls never tried to befriend me, but the teasing and the taunting stopped.

At home while all of this was happening, I was in a query. I didn't want to give up Jesus, but I didn't want to be treated like a plague at school either. I really didn't want to look and feel like a fool when I was asked about my faith. So I began to think about my faith, ask questions and research the Bible. I knew I believed. I just wanted to know why I believed. I spent hours and hours reading, listening, crying, and praying trying to figure out an intelligent answer as to why I was a Christian. One message that kept coming back to me was that Jesus loved me, and He would protect me and that standing up for His name was the right thing to do, even when it was hard. I also knew Jesus was the way to heaven, and heaven seemed like such a wonderful place to be. I didn't want to miss out on the opportunity to go there one day. Especially when so many dear ones that I loved had already gone to heaven. I never went to school and talked about Jesus at all for those first two years of my teenage life. I just wanted to survive. I was still seeking Him in the safety of my home and my church. Until the day my life was threatened, I was scared and didn't know what to say. What came out of my mouth surprised even me. Looking back now, I know it was the Holy Spirit speaking on my behalf through my own mouth. I was scared, but I was bold. I was crying in fear, but I wouldn't back down. I am telling you it was God.

Things changed for me that day. I began to be bolder with my faith and the profession of God's love. I had small bits of bravery at first and then more and more as the years went by. I was reading God's word, praying and listening to sermons at church enough that I began to have answers for my faith. When people would question me about God, I would give an answer. Things were changing. People were changing. I knew, then, how valuable it was to be ready with an answer.

It was the most peaceful and kindest way I knew to battle the unbelief of people around. I also discovered that the hardest and cruelest of people found it difficult to be mean toward genuine kindness.

Being a teenage warrior was great practice for a future life as a warrior. However, I found that battling fellow teens as a teenager was nothing to the battles I faced as an adult. Satan is a vicious and relentless enemy, and he had me crouched in a corner with my hands over my head begging him to stop. He would never stop, and much like the scene in the locker room where the young girl threatened to take my life, I found that Satan would not stop until I stood against him and shouted, "You have no power over me. I love Jesus, and that is a good thing. I am going to live, and I am not going to die. You have to leave me alone. In the name of Jesus, you must stop!"

That is when I began to collect my Swords. The scriptures that would battle Satan when he would attack me. They were my proof that God wins and Satan has already lost. I began to write them out, so I could have them close at hand, ready to use at any given moment. Sheets and sheets of scriptures written out on all the areas of life that I was having struggles. I had dozens of scriptures on "fear free living". I had almost as many scriptures on "provision and protection". We were in great debt, and I lived in fear that we would never be able to come out of that debt. I gathered all the scriptures that proved to me that I had a hope that our lives would not always be in a pit.

In fact, once I felt like our debt was a huge giant hanging over our head, and it was ready to consume us. So I took all our bills and I placed them in a chair and I talked to them just as if it was a "real" giant challenging me. "You have no control over us. You are a bully, and God is going to bring you down. God has promised to protect us and to prosper us. He has given to us pressed down shaken together and running over. God has promised to provide for us according to His riches in glory through Christ Jesus and because God has promised this, you are as nothing. I will give you no authority in our life, for God has all authority." I felt a little ridiculous talking to my bills that way, but it was very liberating. Every month I would put those bills in a chair and profess, "You will not win. God has won, and you are paid off in full by the power of God."

When bad news came our way, I would say... "Yes, but God..." and give some type of scripture that would prove that God was in control. It may look like we don't have enough money to get groceries today, BUT "My God said He will provide all my need according to His riches in glory through Christ Jesus", and "I have never seen the righteous forsaken, nor his seed begging bread." I did not focus on what my eyes saw but what God's Word would say about that situation.

Pretty soon all these papers that I was keeping notes on and writing my promises on were falling out of my Bible, and I was losing some of them. So I made a decision. My Bible would be my tool. I could write the notes in my Bible, and the scriptures were already there. It would be my "working" Bible, so to speak. It would help me be ready at any given moment to fight off the enemy exactly where he was attacking.

I began to "tab" my Bible to show me exactly where my power scriptures were. I could access them at a moment's notice. Here is how it works:

STEP 1: Depending on the size of your Bible, you should pick 3-4 categories of issues that are important to you. Remember this is your Bible, so these subjects should be selected to fight your personal battles. Be specific enough that you understand exactly what you are looking for when you go back to them as references. Categories could be:

Fear-free living

Wisdom

God's love

Forgiveness

Provision/protection

Faithful living

Healing

Children

Worthy/valued

<u>STEP 2:</u> When you have done your research and you have the swords that will help your fight, go to your Bible and "tab" your scripture. You will need something like "Post It" tabs. I prefer the small tabs not flags. I don't like them to collapse into the pages of the Bible. Keep your tabs very orderly. Physical clutter is fatiguing, and you don't want your Bible to look cluttered. Line up your tabs in a row by color and make each color represent a category of scriptures. Write the scripture reference on the tab. Then highlight the scripture in your Bible, so your eye is immediately taken to the right place.

Write the categories meanings on a piece of paper and tape it on the inside of your bible cover. Or write it directly into the bible. IE:

Red: Fear-free living

Blue: Provision

Yellow: Wisdom

That way, when you need a scripture fast and you cannot pull one out of your head from memory, you have a quick reference to the words that are going to help you battle, stand and believe.

STEP 3: Write down your thoughts in your Bible that clarify the piece of scripture to you, so that in the future when you are reading, you are reminded of your discovery. Remember this is your "working" Bible. For instance:

I wrote this in my Bible next to *1 Corinthians 13:4-8* when I came to this great understanding. GOD=LOVE. The verse states.

4Love is patient, love is kind. It does not envy, it does not boast, it is not proud. **5**It does not dishonor others, it is not self-seeking, it is not easily angered, it keeps no record of wrongs. **6**Love does not delight in evil but rejoices with the truth. **7**It always protects, always trusts, always hopes, always perseveres.

8Love never fails.

So then I will go back at times and re-read this scripture replacing the word LOVE with the word GOD.

4God is patient, God is kind. God does not envy, God does not boast, God is not proud. **5**God does not dishonor others, God is not self-seeking, God is not easily angered, God keeps no record of wrongs. **6**God does not delight in evil but rejoices with the truth. **7**God always protects, always trusts, always hopes, always perseveres. **8**God never fails.

This is a way to understand the Word more personally. It makes Bible reading a journey and a treasure hunt, rather than a religious task.

Tabbing your Bible, underlining, and taking notes in your Bible are all activities that you can engage in to make yourself more prepared and ready to give an answer for your faith. It is also a great way to equip your soul and bring it into agreement with God's word. The more you understand what you believe, the more prepared you are to face the world and fight off the enemy.

Make your Bible your friend. Read it. Ask God for understanding and for His wisdom. He has said, if you ask for wisdom, He will give it in abundance. So go ahead and ask. God is ready to give wisdom to you today!

CHAPTER 9

Debriefing with the General

"Give ear to my words, O LORD, Consider my meditation.
{2} Give heed to the voice of my cry, My King and my
God, For to You I will pray. {3} My voice You shall hear
in the morning, O LORD; In the morning I will direct
it to You, And I will look up." Psalms 5:1-3 NKJV

"Good morning, Lord. How are You this morning?"

"I AM doing wonderful. I AM feeling strong and mighty
and full of Love."

"I know it is true. That is one of the things I love about
You most. You are so constant. I always know what to expect
when I spend my time with You. You are always so kind and
welcoming. My morning coffee with You is truly my favorite
time of the day. It is the time of day that gets me charged and
ready to go. I wouldn't miss it for anything. It is so much better
than getting beat up by the enemy every morning. Thank you
for making this time so peaceful and pleasurable."

"You're welcome my girl. I love your thanksgivings."

"I have to admit, however, that some days when our coffee time is over, I get a little nervous about what the rest of the day holds. In fact I get out and out fearful some days. I wish I could just have coffee with You all day long."

"Child, you know that you can talk to Me at any given time of any given day. I AM always here for you. It is okay to stop and pray with Me in the middle of your workday."

"I know God, and I do. In fact, You know that I do that. Granted, it is something new, and I haven't done it for very long. I am talking about the fear I feel when I know I have to leave our alone time together. I am so happy and peaceful in Your presence. I know that when I close your Word, the day has to start with all of its busyness. Sometimes I feel so anxious, and I want the day to be over before it has even started."

"My child, I do know what you are talking about. Overcoming this fear will take you into a new level of awareness of Me. You say you know that I never leave you or forsake you, but do you really KNOW this to be true. You agree with this statement in your mind, but now it is time to believe in your heart. That fact must become your new reality. I NEVER leave you. All day long I AM with you to love on you and protect you. I AM so close that I AM part of you. I AM in you. I AM less than a prayer away, and I AM always here."

"You are right God. My mind is aware that everything You say is true, and it saddens me that my emotions do not always line up with this reality. My spirit is full of you, but my emotions constantly betray me. I have feelings of anxiety that most often turn into fear. Sometimes I even feel overwhelming sadness right after I have finished something that has brought me incredible joy. It just doesn't make sense. It feels as if my emotions are stronger than my thoughts, and I hate that I cannot get control over them. Maybe You could help me in that way?"

"Dear one, of course I can help you. That is what I AM here for. First, I want to ask you, how is your belief?

My belief..?

Yes, your belief. I know you are reading My Word and you are confessing out loud every day, especially when you are in the middle of an attack. I have even noticed that you have recorded My promises on your phone and are listening to them as you go to sleep at night. I think that is pretty special and highly effective. It seems to help you sleep better. Satan is much less likely to attack you when My promises are filling the air. But in all of these things you are doing, do you really believe?"

"God, I love how candid you are with me. You really don't beat around the bush do You? To be quite honest with you, I want to believe everything that I am saying is true, but there is an inward battle within me on many of the scriptures I quote. There are some things that I do not doubt at all, like Your serenity and Your omnipotence. I believe with all my mind that You are the Creator and that You live in all times.

I know You are in control of every situation. I believe that every creature in this universe will one day bow down to Your Mighty Hand. Where I struggle is knowing that all of Your mightiness is in me. I know that You can do all things, but I struggle believing that You can do all things through me. When I read the words, "I can do all things through Christ (the Anointed One) Who gives me strength", *Philippians 4:13* there is a little voice in me that says, "Yes, but…" Every time I hear that voice say, "Yes, but…" I cringe. I know that it is a contradicting voice in me that is creating so much turmoil, and I don't know how to shut it up. I want to believe God. I really do. I just don't know how to genuinely cross over and truly believe, without doubt. Please help me."

"My precious one, you are so sweet. I love you so much. I see your tears, and I know your heart. I have seen your struggles. I have been waiting for you to give Me permission to help. I have been waiting for you to ask. I will never force you to let Me help, but when you seek Me, I will be found. When you ask of Me, I will give Myself to you openly and willingly. It is important that you know where your help comes from. If I helped you without you asking, then there would be a day that you might think, "my success is through my might and my power." You would forget that I had anything to do with your victories. I know there are times when you think that it is your skills that have helped you in life, but now you are aware that you are not capable of helping yourself. I know you want to believe in My power. I will now help you in your unbelief. Because you are seeking Me, you now know where your source of power comes from.

Your trust in Me releases My power to help you believe in your life. You will now begin to believe as I believe, and your thoughts transition to think the way I think. This is a whole new level of living my friend, and I AM excited to take this journey with you."

"Oh God my God! I am so unworthy of all your love and care. And all I can do is thank you. I thank you over and over again. I know my life is in your hands and that is a peaceful place to be. So now, what do you want me to do?"

"Well, at this point I want you to keep coming to me during your coffee time. It seems to be the time you are the most aware of my presence. Every time you come to Me, I will make you more and more aware of who I AM and what My desires are for your life. The biggest goal I have for you, my child, is that you begin to know My Heart. When you know My Heart, you will know Me fully. That will transform your soul, and your actions will follow. Just watch, in the middle of this journey your heart will begin to be filled with joy unspeakable and full of My Glory. It is a wonderful experience. In fact, I will give you so much of My joy that your little heart will not be able to contain it all. It will pour out of you like living water, and it is going to splash onto all that come near you. They will love the way they feel when they are around you, not because of you, sweet one, but because they are seeing and feeling Me through you. This is how I will glorify Myself with your life.

It is a moment by moment thing. Your life will begin to transform one day at a time, one moment at a time. When I ask you to believe, I am asking you to believe for a moment. Then that moment will turn into two moments put together. You will have strong belief for short moments. I will give you opportunities to practice believing. Each time you have an opportunity to reach out to Me in belief, you will be practicing believing. The moments will stretch and become longer in length. I will begin to ask you to believe for longer periods of time, and each time you will grow stronger and stronger in your faith and belief in Me. Then, you will begin to see me working. Each time you see a victory, you grow more and more confident in your belief, until one day you will ONLY BELIEVE!"

"Wow God! That sounds magnificent. It sounds like a great blueprint to live my life by. It sounds like a divine plan and I cannot wait to get started."

"Why wait little one? Let's get started today! This is a practice and your practice starts right now."

"Okay, here we go, God. I can do all things through Christ who gives me strength. I believe and thank You God that you are helping me in my unbelief. I believe fully and completely that your great hand is at work in my life at this very moment. I will not pay attention to what my physical eyes see. I will only focus my eyes on the Word of God. And for today, at this very moment, I ONLY BELIEVE. I am a warrior, and this is the Warrior Way!"

CHAPTER 10

VICTORY!!

The Whole Armor of God

Ephesians 6

[10] Finally, be strong in the Lord and in the strength of his might. [11] Put on the whole armor of God, that you may be able to stand against the schemes of the devil. [12] For we do not wrestle against flesh and blood, but against the rulers, against the authorities, against the cosmic powers over this present darkness, against the spiritual forces of evil in the heavenly places. [13] Therefore take up the whole armor of God, that you may be able to withstand in the evil day, and having done all, to stand firm. [14] Stand therefore, having fastened on the belt of truth, and having put on the breastplate of righteousness, [15] and, as shoes for your feet, having put on the readiness given by the gospel of peace. [16] In all circumstances take up the shield of faith, with which you can extinguish all the flaming darts off the evil one; [17] and take the helmet of salvation, and the sword of the Spirit, which is the word of God, [18] praying at all times in the Spirit, with all prayer and supplication."

Leanne McDougall

This is your Whole Armor of God.

Truth is found in the Word and through the Spirit.

Righteousness: God's Spirit is perfect in righteousness. His Spirit is in your spirit therefore, if you are saved, you are the righteousness of God.

Gospel of Peace: Know what the bible says. Know the Good News that brings peace. The Good News is the salvation message of Jesus Christ.

Faith: Only believe! And God will help you in your unbelief

Salvation: Confess that Jesus is the sacrifice for your sins. Recognize that He died so that you do not have to die. Receive Him as your Lord, giving Him power and authority over your life.

Sword of the Spirit: It is your Bible. Know it!

Prayer and supplication: Open your mouth and confess.

The final victory. The Christian Faith.

Romans 8 Living Bible (TLB)

"So there is now no condemnation awaiting those who belong to Christ Jesus. [2] For the power of the life-giving Spirit— and this power is mine through Christ Jesus—has freed me from the vicious circle of sin and death. [3] We aren't saved from sin's grasp by knowing the commandments of God because we can't and don't keep them, but God put into effect a different plan to save us. He sent His own Son in a human body like ours—except that ours are sinful—and destroyed sin's control over us by giving Himself as a sacrifice for our sins. ⁴ So now we can obey God's laws if we follow after the Holy Spirit and no longer obey the old evil nature within us.

⁵ Those who let themselves be controlled by their lower natures live only to please themselves, but those who follow after the Holy Spirit find themselves doing those things that please God. ⁶ Following after the Holy Spirit leads to life and peace, but following after the old nature leads to death ⁷ because the old sinful nature within us is against God. It never did obey God's laws and it never will. ⁸ That's why those who are still under the control of their old sinful selves, bent on following their old evil desires, can never please God.

⁹ But you are not like that. You are controlled by your new nature if you have the Spirit of God living in you. (And remember that if anyone doesn't have the Spirit of Christ living in him, he is not a Christian at all.) ¹⁰ Yet, even though Christ lives within you, your body will die because of sin; but your spirit will live, for Christ has pardoned it.[a] ¹¹ And if the Spirit of God, who raised up Jesus from the dead, lives in you, he will make your dying bodies live again after you die, by means of this same Holy Spirit living within you.

¹² So, dear brothers, you have no obligations whatever to your old sinful nature to do what it begs you to do. ¹³ For if

you keep on following it you are lost and will perish, but if through the power of the Holy Spirit you crush it and its evil deeds, you shall live. [14] For all who are led by the Spirit of God are sons of God.

[15] And so we should not be like cringing, fearful slaves, but we should behave like God's very own children, adopted into the bosom of his family, and calling to him, "Father, Father." [16] For his Holy Spirit speaks to us deep in our hearts and tells us that we really are God's children. [17] And since we are his children, we will share his treasures—for all God gives to his Son Jesus is now ours too. But if we are to share his glory, we must also share his suffering.

[18] Yet what we suffer now is nothing compared to the glory he will give us later. [19] For all creation is waiting patiently and hopefully for that future day[b] when God will resurrect his children. [20-21] For on that day thorns and thistles, sin, death, and decay[c]—the things that overcame the world against its will at God's command—will all disappear, and the world around us will share in the glorious freedom from sin which God's children enjoy.

[22] For we know that even the things of nature, like animals and plants, suffer in sickness and death as they await this great event.[d] [23] And even we Christians, although we have the Holy Spirit within us as a foretaste of future glory, also groan to be released from pain and suffering. We, too, wait anxiously for that day when God will give us our full rights as his children,

including the new bodies he has promised us—bodies that will never be sick again and will never die.

²⁴ We are saved by trusting. And trusting means looking forward to getting something we don't yet have—for a man who already has something doesn't need to hope and trust that he will get it. ²⁵ But if we must keep trusting God for something that hasn't happened yet, it teaches us to wait patiently and confidently.

²⁶ And in the same way—by our faith[e]—the Holy Spirit helps us with our daily problems and in our praying. For we don't even know what we should pray for nor how to pray as we should, but the Holy Spirit prays for us with such feeling that it cannot be expressed in words. ²⁷ And the Father who knows all hearts knows, of course, what the Spirit is saying as he pleads for us in harmony with God's own will. ²⁸ And we know that all that happens to us is working for our good if we love God and are fitting into his plans.

²⁹ For from the very beginning God decided that those who came to him—and all along he knew who would—should become like his Son, so that his Son would be the First, with many brothers. ³⁰ And having chosen us, he called us to come to him; and when we came, he declared us "not guilty," filled us with Christ's goodness, gave us right standing with himself, and promised us his glory.

³¹ What can we ever say to such wonderful things as these? If God is on our side, who can ever be against us? ³² Since He

did not spare even His own Son for us but gave Him up for us all, won't he also surely give us everything else?

[33] Who dares accuse us whom God has chosen for His own? Will God? No! He is the One who has forgiven us and given us right standing with Himself.

[34] Who then will condemn us? Will Christ? *No!* For he is the one who died for us and came back to life again for us and is sitting at the place of highest honor next to God, pleading for us there in heaven.

[35] Who then can ever keep Christ's love from us? When we have trouble or calamity, when we are hunted down or destroyed, is it because he doesn't love us anymore? And if we are hungry or penniless or in danger or threatened with death, has God deserted us?

[36] No, for the Scriptures tell us that for his sake we must be ready to face death at every moment of the day—we are like sheep awaiting slaughter; [37] but despite all this, overwhelming victory is ours through Christ who loved us enough to die for us. [38] For I am convinced that nothing can ever separate us from his love. Death can't, and life can't. The angels won't, and all the powers of hell itself cannot keep God's love away. Our fears for today, our worries about tomorrow, [39] or where we are—high above the sky, or in the deepest ocean—nothing will ever be able to separate us from the love of God demonstrated by our Lord Jesus Christ when he died for us."

Amen

Satan cannot stand against you when the Holy Spirit is with you. God has already won the whole war and because He has won, you WIN!!

"WARRIOR, I Salute you!!

"This is my Bible

I have what it says I have

I can do what it says I can do

I am who it says I am

I am more than a conqueror

Through Christ who gives me strength

I am a warrior

And this is the WARRIOR WAY

[24] "Therefore I tell you, whatever you ask for in prayer, believe that you have received it, and it will be yours." Mark 11:24